not a guide to

Southampton

James Marsh

The
History
Press

*This book is dedicated to my son
James, his partner Sarah and my two
grandsons Jayden and Finley*

First published 2013

The History Press
The Mill, Brimscombe Port
Stroud, Gloucestershire, GL5 2QG
www.thehistorypress.co.uk

British Library Cataloguing in Publication Data.
A catalogue record for this book is available from the British Library.

ISBN 978 0 7524 7476 2

Typesetting and origination by The History Press
Printed in Great Britain

Coat of Arms

SOUTHAMPTON.

The coat of arms for Southampton is copyright of the mayor's office and as such can only be used by the mayor. Shown here is a replica. This one, issued in 1894, is black and white and differs from the original (the knight's helmet on the 1575 version is missing and the ships are depicted facing in the opposite direction). No record of the origin of this coat of arms can be found, despite extensive research.

Contents

Foreword

This book is all you remember of Southampton, all you will come to remember in the future, and everything in between. It has made me think of what it means to have been born here, and for me it is a mix of so many things from past and present which make me proud to be a local.

Southampton is, for me, the sum of the memories passed down by my family and those of the people I have been fortunate enough to meet over the years. Stories of trams travelling through the Bargate; the fine buildings before the Blitz; the memories from the war when the city was targeted by the Nazis and the hundreds who died in the Civic Centre shelter that terrible day; the aftermath of the *Titanic* disaster which affected so many in the city, remembered to this day at the *Titanic* Memorial and the SeaCity Museum; the floating bridge before the Itchen Bridge, when it was an adventure to get to town from the eastern side of the river. I also remember the Ocean Terminal, the forerunner to the huge Southampton Cruise Industry today; and South Western House when it was a luxury hotel and latterly housed the BBC; there was also shipbuilding at Vosper Thornycrofts – which is now being redeveloped into housing and marine employment.

I remember the zoo on the Common, the flowerbeds next to Palmerston Park which were planted into words and pictures; the TVS studios by Northam Bridge with the huge banana outside; the ice rink and the Top Rank nightclub. And of course, I remember many Saturdays standing on the terraces at the Dell cheering on the Saints; their promotion to the first division; and I will never forget when we won the FA Cup in 1976; I went out as a boy to wait for the victory bus tour to pass through Bitterne Park Triangle.

This book is a must read for anyone who was born in Southampton or has an interest in the city's rich and varied history. It is a stunning collection of memoirs, photographs and accounts of Southampton through the years.

Councillor Royston Smith, 2013

Acknowledgements

I wish to thank my son James for his help with editing this book, without him I would have struggled in that department; my friend and colleague Penny Legg, whose help and suggestions have proved so valuable in the production of the book; the staff of Southampton's Archives department; David Hollingsworth, and the staff at Southampton Reference Library; Friends of Southampton Old Cemetery; Chris Brunnen, photographer at JCB photography for his aerial photo of Southampton; Julie Green who has supplied so many of the photographs used in the book; Councillor David Shields for all his help; Councillor Royston Smith for his welcome foreword to the book and his help with research; Dawn Tomkins and the legal department of John Lewis; Brian Hooper and Jeff Henry for the words of the song about Southampton; Peter Collins for his ghost stories; SeaCity Museum for the photos supplied; Jim Brown for permission to use murder stories from his book on the subject; Roger Cooper and the Nick Hancock design studio for the wonderful photo of the forthcoming monument to the Spitfire; Exxon Mobil for the superb photograph of Fawley Oil Refinery; and my very good friend Jane Rubin for her help with suggestions and photo sites of old Southampton. Lastly I would like to thank Scott Brownrigg Chartered Architects, and Johnathon Edwards from Morgan Sindal.

ITCHEN ROAD BRIDGE, SOUTHAMPTON

Introduction

When I was asked to write this book I found it a great honour and a privilege, but I realised that I had never done anything like it before. Frankly, at first I was a bit lost and had no idea of how to go about it. But since starting it has been the most amazing fun as I have discovered so much about my home city of Southampton. I thought I knew my city, but boy was I wrong. This has been a trip down the road of discovery for me and I hope it will be the same for you.

James Marsh, 2013

Welcome to Southampton

The town of Southampton became a city after a royal charter in 1964. Coming into Southampton from London this is the first notice that you have arrived. This 'Welcome To' sign is situated at the Chilworth roundabout and leads directly into the Avenue, the main approach into the town centre. But it is not easy to pick up because it is surrounded by much larger signs showing the route into the city.

Southampton

The Saxon town of Hamwic was in the area now known as Northam and St Mary's (where St Mary's church stands today) in around AD 700–850. It was changed to Southampton in later years when King Alfred decided to take action to repel raids by Danish Vikings. They had sacked the town on several occasions, so the king decided to hit back by building fortifications that were known as burghs. All the men of Hamwic were required to report to these whenever danger threatened from Denmark. The burghs were called hamtuns and since Hamwic was in the south it took on the name Southamptun. Later this changed to the name we know today.

A wonderful mural depicting the rise of this city from Clausentum in Roman times through the Saxon period up to present-day Southampton is located on a wall in Hamtun Street. This can be found by leaving the Town Quay and proceeding up Bugle Street. Just past St Michaels Square, Hamtun Street is the second on the right. Also, on the approach to Holyrood church there's a plaque in the pavement informing us that 250 years after the Romans left, the Saxon town of Hamwic was founded on the west bank of the River Itchen.

HAMTUN STREET

City of Southampton

Grid Reference

OS Reference: SU412 121

50.89696°N 1.40416°W

Twinning

Southampton is twinned with Le-Havre, France, since 1973 and Rems-Murr-Kreise, Germany, since 1991.

It is also a sister city to Hampton, Virginia, USA, and Qingdao, China, since 1998.

Aerial Views of Southampton

This photo, courtesy of CJB photography, shows the docks with two cruise liners and one of Cunard's huge *Queens* at their berths. The River Itchen passes St Mary's Stadium, home to Southampton Football Club, before merging with the Test to form Southampton Water. Itchen Bridge replaced the old floating bridges that crossed this river for so many years. The city itself sprawls out beyond the docks, and the downs between Southampton and Winchester are set in a wonderful panorama. The ruined pier is also visible. Hopes are high that something will soon be done to convert this old, crumbling structure into a new and thriving complex, the like of which Southampton's residents have been waiting for.

The second photograph shows the docks around the turn of the twentieth century, highlighting how much this area has changed. This is how it looked in the days of the White Star Line when the *Titanic* set sail on its fateful maiden voyage. Looking down Southampton Water towards the Solent, the far bank is open country. This is where Fawley Refinery now stands. In the forefront of this photo, beyond what looks like a portable dry dock, the Town Quay is also well in view.

Fawley Refinery is also shown here in its present-day setting. Built in 1921, it is now the largest of its kind in the country and has a capacity of 330,000 barrels of crude oil a day, brought here from all around the world.

Street Names

Winkle Street – although I never liked the idea of actually eating winkles, Southampton Water houses some of the most important cockle and winkle beds in the country. Could the street be named after this? Apparently not, in medieval times this street name was spelt wincle. This is an old world word that means nook, corner or angle.

Lumpy Lane – having visited this I can confirm there is nothing lumpy about it at all.

Oxford Street – leads out facing the forecourt of what was once the Terminus railway station. To the left was where the offices of the Shipping Federation stood. It was here that seamen came to be assigned to various ships coming in and out of Southampton Docks, carrying their cargoes to all parts of the world. Also to be found in Oxford Street is the one-time 'home for seamen'. Many coming ashore had nowhere else to stay while they waited to ship out again. Another landmark is the famous public house, The Grapes. Many of the crew of the ill-fated *Titanic* spent time drinking there before joining the ship for its maiden voyage. Many of course, never returned.

Regent Street – it is perhaps nowhere near as opulent as its London counterpart. In fact, it is hard to find; you need to look carefully before entering the pedestrian precinct, looking down towards the Bargate in order to see it. It is a small back alley where goods are delivered to some of the stores on the High Street. It's also used as a shortcut by many who want to get through to Portland Terrace and on down to West Quay shopping centre.

A Snapshot of Southampton Wards

The city of Southampton is divided into many wards, which all fall in one or other of the two parliamentary constituencies of Itchen and Test.

Bitterne has a population of around 13,000 and takes in places such as Lances Hill and the Bitterne shopping precinct. Large housing areas are found here such as Townhill Park. The area is linked with Northam by Northam Bridge, and at the other side Cobden Bridge connects it with St Denys.

Harefield is a suburb near to Bitterne and is well known for the very large council estate that dominates it.

Sholing is an area that is in between Bitterne and Thornhill and boasts good schools as well as Itchen College. It is a large area with a well-known sports ground in Spring Road, a wide open piece of land enjoyed by sportsmen and children alike for generations.

Woolston is now linked to downtown Southampton by the Itchen toll bridge. Opened in 1977, this bridge was long awaited by the residents of Woolston because the only means of crossing the River Itchen at this point was the floating bridge. Pedestrians could travel free on these floating bridges that were pulled across the river on powerful cables, but cars vans and motor bikes were charged a small amount. Lorries and busses, however, could not be accommodated. Woolston is a wide area with well-known streets and decent shopping facilities.

Bargate ward takes in the city centre precinct and the old walls, the old part of town below the Bargate with the city vaults that date back many centuries, and Southampton's oldest public house, the Red Lion.

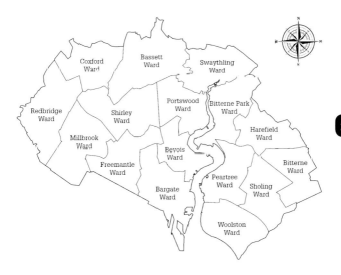

St Mary's, dominated by the historic St Mary's church, is also home to Southampton City College. The church, which is next door to the college, was the origin of Southampton Football Club, which started life as Southampton Saint Marys; it has given the club its nickname: the Saints. Ocean Village on Canute Road is a haven for yachts and a joy to visit. It is said that King Canute sat here when he commanded the tide to go back. Holyrood church, bombed during the war, is in this old part of town as well and is now kept in its ruined state as a shrine to seaman. One of the *Titanic* memorials is to be found here also. The polygon area of this ward once boasted one of Southampton's best-known hotels; situated just north of the railway station in Commercial Road and bounded by Watts Park, the Polygon Hotel dominated the skyline. Many famous people stayed here, as well as passengers waiting to board the *Titanic* in 1912. Sadly the hotel was demolished as demands for modern facilities mounted – the site is now a block of flats.

Bevois Valley, which also takes in Bevois town, is the area very near to Portswood Junction. It is popular with students for accommodation, as it is within walking distance of Southampton University. The very old church that was once St Luke's, which stood on the corner of Cranbury Avenue, is now a Sikh temple known as Singh Sabha Gurdwara.

Nichcolstown, also known as Newtown, lies to the north-east of the city centre.

Northam, in the east, encompasses famous areas like Six Dials and the Royal South Hants Hospital. Northam itself, to the east of Nichcolstown is dominated by Northam Bridge which connects it with Bitterne. Many old famous public houses are found here. This area was worst hit in 1912 as many crew members from RMS *Titanic* lived in the area.

Freemantle and **Shirley** are areas that I know best, having lived in and around them for many years.

This is not the full list of the many suburbs and wards in this great city. But I have covered those that I think will be best known to many people who, like me, are Sotonians.

Distance from:

	Miles	Km
Ayers Rock, Australia	8,684	13,977
Brussels, Belgium	298	480
Centre of the Earth (approx.)	3,947	6,353
Eiffel Tower, Paris	249	400
Los Angeles, USA	5,440	8,752
Frankfurt, Germany	548	882
Glasgow, Scotland	362	582
Hong Kong, China	6,036	9,744
Istanbul, Turkey	1,593	2,563
Jerusalem, Israel	2,284	3,675
The Kremlin, Russia	1,616	2,600
Machu Pichu, Peru	5,836	9,390
The Moon (approx.)	238,857	384,403
Niagara Falls, North America	3,535	5,687
Seoul, South Korea	5,572	8,695
San Nicolas, Aruba	4,618	7,430
New York, USA	3,424	5,509
Vatican City	906	1,457

24 Hours in Southampton

05.30-06.00   Dock workers and paper boys rise and begin their days' work.

7.00-9.00   Office workers trundle along to their offices, as the rare early morning student makes their way to morning lectures.

10.00   The Tudor House Museum and SeaCity Museum open their doors.

11.00   The cities libraries start to get busy as readers and lenders trickle in.

13.00   Ships go out from Southampton's busy docks.

15.00   Southampton F.C. face their Premiership rivals each Saturday.

18.00-19.00   The evening commute starts in earnest as the city's busy bus lines crowd the streets to take home weary heads.

21.00   Bars and clubs start to fill up as people journey out to sample Southampton's famous nightlife.

00.00   The Civic Centre bell chimes the hour to signal the day's end.

03.00   Bars and clubs close as students head home to prepare for the following collegial day.

Southampton International

Southampton is located in south-eastern Suffolk County, New York, USA. The town contains a diminutive village named after the Earl of Southampton. Come summer the town is filled with the super wealthy from New York who have holiday homes there.

There is a small community, roughly 3,083 people, called Southampton in Ontario, Canada.

Southampton Island is a large island at the entrance to Hudson Bay in north-eastern Canada. It is one of the larger members of the Canadian Arctic Archipelago, and is part of the Kivalliq Region in Nunavut.

There is also Southampton homestead in the south-west of Western Australia, It is a small Victorian-Georgian historical homestead located on the banks of the Blackwood river.

The Red Lion Public House

At No. 55 High Street, just down the road from Holyrood church, there is a remarkable old pub dating back to 1148. Sandwiched between the Grade II* listed building, now operating as Junnes Indian Restaurant, and the modern building on the other side trading as Mack, the Red Lion sits in the oldest part of Southampton. So many people walking past this site have no idea of the amazing history of this building.

I had the pleasure of meeting Tony and Tish Morris who have been running it for the past eleven years, and Tish held me spellbound with tales of its ghostly side and of the famous trial held here in 1415. As we sat in the bar just before opening time the present-day landlady told me about the ghost hunts and other happenings that go on:

> I was here one day and a chap came up and asked me what the door downstairs was. I told him it was the garage. He said it couldn't be because he could hear someone snoring in there. I said that was impossible but he insisted on finding out what this was all about. He was running a ghost night here so I couldn't really refuse him, and as my seventeen-year-old son told me he had always wanted to do this I said alright, get the keys then.

Welcom... ...d Linn

Henry V Court Room

Scene Of The Trial Of Those Who
Conspired Against The Life & Crown
Of Henry V In 1415, Prior To Henry's
Departure To Agincourt
The Conspiritors Were Found Guilty &
Executed Outside The Nearby Bargate

Southampton

So my son and at least four members of the ghost hunt went down there and I said I would open the door and go in first because I knew where the light switch was. The man who started this stood just to the right of the entrance. As I turned the key however, the door flew open and something came rushing out and knocked all of us off of our feet. I was asked afterwards what I had seen and could only describe it as a great ball of white light. My son went scrambling over backwards then, gaining his feet, rushed back inside the pub, only coming back when he realised his mum wasn't with him. That, I have to say, must be the weirdest thing that has happened to me here.

There is a ghost downstairs who we know as Bruce, many ghost hunters here have seen him and all describe this man in exactly the same way, so there must be something in it. They all say his attitude isn't very nice at all, I would say he is arrogant and one of the chaps I know once said, 'I'm going down and I'll wind Bruce up a bit.' When he came back up though he was as white as a sheet, he told me Bruce had told him to 'get out before I hurt you'. And this man, who had done ghost hunts all over the place, said this had to be the most frightening thing he has ever experienced.

There is a little boy who stands at the top of the stairs and I was told by a medium he was unhappy I had got rid of a member of staff he liked. This was a family member I had argued with and sacked two weeks before. I had to phone up and say come back because the little boy is sad without you. So many mediums and ghost hunters have had amazing results in here and I would really love to see a ghost myself, though how I would react if I did I don't know.

So if you want to experience the warm atmosphere and welcome given to all customers by Tish and Tony call in at the Red Lion. Who knows, you might see the lady who floats along the top balcony and sometimes stands behind the bar. The little boy may smile at you but watch out for surly Bruce!

Southampton in Song

Two of my favourite of Southampton's musical sons are Brian Hooper and Jeff Henry. According to their website:

> Brian is the long standing MC of the Fo'c'sle club. He has been on the folk scene in Southampton and surrounding areas for more years than he can, or may care to remember.

> Jeff has been performing a wide range of songs around the folk clubs of Southampton since the early 1970s, either singing acapella or accompanying himself on guitar. The original idea for a CD specifically featuring songs about Southampton came from Brian who thought if New York and Chicago warranted songs about them, then so did his home town as well.

Several local songwriters had chosen the city as subject matter, and further delving uncovered more. Brian and Jeff decided it was their turn to apply their song-writing talents to this musical legacy. Their album 'Southampton in Song' is the result.

I had the pleasure of meeting Brian at his home and during a most interesting talk he told me more about himself and the album that he and Jeff have produced. Born and raised in Portsmouth, Brian came to Southampton in 1972 after marrying. He overcame the perennial rivalry between the Royal Navy town and the maritime city of Southampton and wanted to highlight just what a wonderful place Southampton, with such a rich heritage, is to live. I bought a copy and have laughed but also been humbled at the history that is spelt out in song.

By kind permission of Brian I reproduce the words of this last song, because for me it sums up so beautifully the wonders of the place in which I was born and bred.

Here in Southampton

He who would cheerful be, seaman or landsman,
Let him come here and see my home Southampton;
Some folk they talk it down, I will not share their frown,
I'm proud this is my town, here in Southampton.

Ocean Village, fancy yachts, bought at the boat show;
West Quay and all those shops, Mayflower Panto;
Turner Simms and Harbour Lights, Red Jet to the Isle
of Wight;
Craig David, he's alright here in Southampton.

Knights of the Bowling Green, Bargate on Mayday;
Oriana, Solent Scene, cruise or awayday;
Quarterjacks at holyrood, knick-knacks from Northam
Road
Jumpin Jack's at Leisure World, here in Southampton.

We've a common, fair and green, armies have camped on;
Folks of every race and creed at home in Southampton;
Angling at Weston Shore, sunset in St Michael's Square,
Ships' horns to welcome in the year, here in
Southampton.

Red and white the colours to wear, watching the
Saints play;
Ghosts of legends fill the air, Channon, Le Tissier,
Whether we lose or win, you'll always hear us sing
When the Saints go marching in, here in Southampton.

Though you travel far and near, Eastleigh or
Bournemouth,
There's none that can compare, Gosport or Portsmouth
Pride of the Hampshire coast, the town we love the most,

We'll drink a hearty toast, here's to Southampton.

How Many Times a Year?

Every year on Southampton Common in July there is a race for life. Women of all ages run in this to raise funds and awareness of cancer.

The fair also comes to the Common three times a year – on Easter, May Day and August bank holidays. In my youth these were the most exciting of times. Riding on the big wheel and dodgems, known to us as bumper cars, were great favourites. More recently the Southampton Show was a highlight enjoyed by countless thousands of visitors each year. This eventually gave way to the Southampton Balloon Festival and I have very fond memories of being at the showground early in the morning, watching these balloons being inflated and eventually taking off. When weather permitted the sky over Southampton was a sight to behold with hot air balloons floating across it.

At the other end of the city Mayflower Park, site of the former pier, hosts the annual Boat Show. This is among the largest of its kind in the country. Just how much money changes hands here every year can only be wondered at. The Boat Show lunch is held annually at the De Veer Grand Harbour Hotel, where the ticket price includes entrance to the show.

At the Bargate, once the gateway to the town and a very prominent structure in the middle of the High Street, a ceremony is conducted at first light on May Day. A choir climbs to the top and sings hymns, while a team of morris dancers perform in front.

Two ceremonies from the mayoral calendar can be attended by the public. The Mayor Making ceremony at the Guild Hall in May and the Remembrance Day parade at the Cenotaph in November.

Did You Know?

Southampton can claim fame as the first city to sample fish fingers. In the 1930s an attempt was made to make herring more appealing to people. The fish was presented in sticks and labelled as herring savouries. These were tested against another similar product, using cod, which they called fish fingers. The tests took place in South Wales and Southampton and the cod won easily. Southampton can therefore be proud of the part it played. This would lead to the ever-popular fish fingers, produced in Great Yarmouth, being introduced to the whole of Great Britain in 1955.

If you turn off the High Street and walk down Ogle Road you may easily miss a little plaque on the wall. This serves as a reminder of the Hippodrome Theatre, which was popular in the early twentieth century. It was here in, 1911, that the famous escapologist Harry Houdini first performed his Chinese Water Torture trick. This was introduced on the last day of a week-long run of shows and the charge to see it was one guinea. This was such a lot of money that only one person agreed to pay it. Houdini was delighted though because that's all he needed. Many of his escapes were being duplicated by other artists, but if just one person saw him perform the trick he could patent it for himself.

It was also right here in Southampton that King Canute famously commanded the waves to go back. He was fed up with his courtiers telling him how great he was so decided to show them not everything obeyed his commands. The sea certainly didn't, and he got more than his feet wet as it swept up to where he was sitting. This is believed to be on the site now occupied by Ocean Village in the appropriately named Canute Road.

Famous for ...

The Spitfire – a plaque commemorating the creator of the Spitfire fighter plane, R.J. Mitchell, is placed very close to the Itchen Bridge, where the factory that produced the plane was situated. The bridge itself was not there in those days. Instead floating bridges went back and forth across the Itchen connecting Woolston with downtown Southampton. The first prototype of the Spitfire, code named K5054, took off from Eastleigh Aerodrome, now Southampton Airport, on 5 March 1935. At the controls was experienced test pilot Joseph Mutt-Summers. This aircraft was to prove successful during the Second World War and won the battle with the German Luftwaffe.

Southampton Docks – the docks played a major role in the preparation and departure of troops on D-Day. The build-up was huge and they were filled with craft of all sorts before the invasion fleet set sail on 6 June 1944. This heralded the end of the war in Europe. The Docks are still a large part of life in Southampton, with famous liners from all over the world coming and going on a regular basis. I grew up during the time of the two Cunard liners, *Queen Mary* and *Queen Elizabeth*. So many stars of stage and screen entered this country from one or the other of these ships. Numerous newspaper cuttings show them waving from the decks. The *Titanic* set sail from here on 10 April 1912 and many reminders of this great ship are situated in Southampton to this day.

Cruise ships – Southampton today is still a very important cruise port, home to three of Cunard's massive liners, *Queen Mary 2*, *Queen Elizabeth* and *Queen Victoria*. These have taken over from the *QE2* that sailed for so many years, coming into service when the first two *Queens* were retired. Add the huge container terminal as well and the importance of Southampton Docks, with its four tides a day, is easy to see.

TO THE MEMORY OF THOSE WOOLSTON WORKERS KILLED & INJURED BY ENEMY BOMBING AT THE SUPERMARINE WORKS NEAR THIS SITE ON 24 AND 26 SEPTEMBER 1940 AND TO RECORD WITH PRIDE THE LONG LINE OF FAMOUS AIRCRAFT DESIGNED AND BUILT HERE BY SOUTHAMPTON PEOPLE

SCHNEIDER TROPHY SEAPLANE
SOUTHAMPTON
SCAPA
STRANRAER
WALRUS
SEAGULL
SPITFIRE

THIS PLAQUE WAS DEDICATED BY THE REVEREND CANON R.B. WHEELER, RECTOR OF SOUTHAMPTON ON THE SIXTIETH ANNIVERSARY OF THE MAIDEN FLIGHT OF THE SPITFIRE 5 MARCH 1936

Most Expensive
and Beautiful Buildings

The Prudential Assurance building has stood on Southampton High Street for many years and is a familiar sight to residents of the city. Converted into flats, the brown front of this imposing structure has always filled me with pride every time I pass it.

The Church of St Michael's, standing in its own square, is not only one of the oldest buildings in the city, dating from 1070, but also one of the most elegant. An impressive spire rising 165ft helped ensure its survival during the Blitz and the continued bombing that Southampton suffered from the German Luftwaffe until 1944. It is believed that pilots were instructed not to bomb the church because the high spire could be used for direction. St Michael's is one of the oldest public buildings in the city.

Holyrood was not so fortunate. During the night of 30 November 1940, when so much of Southampton's High Street was destroyed by German bombs, this beautiful church was hit and almost totally destroyed.

Home-grown Companies

Southampton was once the home of Thornycrofts shipbuilders in Woolston. This became Vosper Thornycrofts after its merger with Vosper's Ltd of Portsmouth in 1966. Many small naval craft were built in this yard and it was a familiar sight to people crossing the Itchen on the old floating bridge. The company has now moved to Portsmouth and the site it occupied is being developed as a housing complex.

The Ford Motor Company can be found in Wide Lane, Swaythling, and has been producing the transit van for many years as well as cabs for the A series trucks. The site was formerly Briggs Motor Bodies. During the Second World War, Spitfire parts were assembled in this factory.

The Thorn Press is an independent publisher based in Southampton. It is run by Tessa Lorant Warburg who is a member of Writing Buddies. This group for writers, led by Penny Legg, meets at the Art house Gallery Café once a month on Friday afternoons. The Thorn Press has published several *Heritage of Knitting* pattern books, written by Tessa herself.

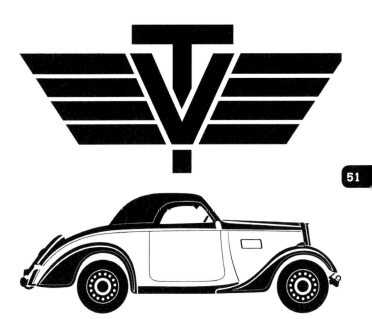

Famous Southampton People

Jane Austen (1775–1817) lived in Southampton from 1807 until 1809. Her house had a garden that backed up to the old walls and the sea waves came right up to this at full tide. She famously danced in the elegant ballroom of the Dolphin Hotel in the High Street below the Bargate. A well-known pub now stands where Jane's house used to be. This was known as the Juniper Berry for many years until a change of name came about and it became the Boson's Locker. The present landlord and landlady have changed it back again so the Juniper Berry now stands proud behind the old walls.

Benny Hill (1924–1992) was born in Southampton, grew up in the city and attended Taunton's School. During his career as a brilliant television comedian he moved away, preferring to rent a home in London where he could be nearer the studio. He did, however, keep the family home on Westrow Gardens and often came back. It wasn't unusual when walking down Southampton High Street to see Benny walking the other way carrying his shopping, as he never owned a car. He is buried here in Hollybrook Cemetery.

CITY OF SOUTHAMPTON

JANE AUSTEN
AUTHOR: 1775-1817

JANE AUSTEN'S HOUSE

JANE'S HOME FROM 1807 TO 1809 WAS SITED
HERE IN CASTLE SQUARE. THE HOUSE WAS
RENTED FROM THE MARQUIS OF LANSDOWNE,
WHO LIVED OPPOSITE IN HIS MOCK-GOTHIC
CASTLE. THE AUSTEN'S GARDEN STRETCHED
BACK TO THE TOWN WALLS, AFFORDING
EXTENSIVE VIEWS OF THE NEW FOREST.
AT THAT TIME THE RIVER TEST, AT HIGH
TIDE, REACHED THE BASE OF THE WALLS.

Craig David was born in Southampton on 5 May 1981. He is now known around the world as a talented singer-songwriter. David has a deservedly large fan following and Southampton is proud of its famous son.

Sir John Everett Millais (1829–1896) was born in Southampton. He trained at the Royal Academy of Art and became well-known as a painter and illustrator.

Gordon of Khartoum (1833–1885) was born in London but came to Southampton with his family in 1857. They lived in an elegant house at No. 5 Rockstone Place. The general came to look on this as his permanent home whenever he had the chance to return from his many exploits abroad. The house now has a plaque on the wall dedicated to the Gordon household. A memorial can be found in Queens Park.

Sir Sidney Kimber (1873–1949) was Mayor of Southampton for two consecutive terms, from November 1918 to November 1920. Then, as an alderman, he was involved in the construction of the Civic Centre and Southampton Sports Centre.

Lord Maybury King (1901–1986) was born on Teesside, studied at King's College, London, and then came to Southampton in 1922, where he taught at Taunton's School. For seventeen years he held the position of Head of English before becoming headmaster at Regents Park School. Entering politics with an unsuccessful attempt to capture the New Forest seat for Labour in 1945, he went on to win both Southampton constituencies – Itchen and then Test. He was the first Labour MP to become Speaker of the House of Commons and lived on Manor Farm Road.

Chris Packham was born in Southampton on 4 May 1961. He is a naturalist, nature photographer and television presenter. Educated in Southampton at Richard Taunton's College he later became known for his television appearances. These include the Bafta-award winning children's programme *The Really Wild Show*, *Wild Shots*, *The X Creatures*, *Hands on Nature* and *Nature's Calendar*. In June 2009 he became co-presenter of *Spring Watch* and *Autumn Watch* alongside Kate Humble. He is president of the Hampshire-based charities The Hawk Conservancy Trust and the Bat Conservancy Trust. He is also vice-president of the Royal Society for the Protection of Birds among many others. In 2011 he was awarded the British Trust for Ornithology medal. He is patron of the Woolston Eyes Conservation Group which manages Woolston Eyes Bird Reserve.

N.J. Crisp (1923–2005) television writer, dramatist and novelist, was an old Tauntonian who was born in Southampton. After service in the RAF he was, for a time, manager of Streamline Taxis before turning to his main interest, writing. He got his big break with the BBC with a thriller entitled *People of the Night*. A decade later he won a Writers' Guild of Great Britain award, and a Best Writer of British TV award for his contributions to *Dixon of Dock Green*, *Dr Finlay's Casebook* and others of note. He lived in Abbots Way Highfield.

Ken Russell (1927–2011) was born in Southampton. He is well known for directing *The Devils*, *The Who's Tommy*, *Altered States* and the Oscar-nominated *Women in Love*. He has also made films about famous composers among which are: Elgar, Delius, Liszt, and Tchaikovsky.

Parks and Open Spaces

Southampton is blessed with seven major, beautiful parks that make it the greenest city in the south of England. Approaching the Town Junction opposite the municipal library and art gallery is Watts Park. Here amongst the greenery and wonderful flower beds, is a statue of Isaac Watts (1674–1748) who was a well-known writer of hymns as well as an accomplished author.

In Watts Park there is a concrete structure named the Tower. It is a monument to architect Ernest Berry Webber, whose designs were chosen for the Civic Centre. At the other end, opposite the monument to the engineers who perished aboard the *Titanic*, is Southampton's magnificent Cenotaph. Designed by Sir Edwin Lutyens it is inscribed with the quotation: 'Their Name Liveth Forever'. It was unveiled and dedicated on 6 November 1920.

Andrews Park, known to many as East Park, is on the other side of the road. Here you will find the statue of Richard Andrews (1798–1859), coachbuilder and former Mayor of Southampton for three consecutive years from 1849. You will also see the beautiful Queens Peace Fountain. A flower-decked walkway leads down into the park which is a riot of colour during the spring and summer months.

Palmerstone Park is divided from Houndwell Park by Pound Tree Road. In these beautiful parks a bandstand is to be found as well as a gas column erected to the memory of William Chamberlayne who was MP for Southampton from 1818 to 1829.

Opposite Debenhams department store, once known as Edwin Jones, is Hoglands Park. A skateboard track is used frequently by young people and sports such as cricket and football are played here. Many parts of Southampton are, unfortunately, adorned by terrible graffiti, but in Hoglands Park there is a building painted in this style that looks extremely decorative as a result.

Mayflower Park is situated alongside what is left of the once lovely pier. From here ships can be seen coming and going from Southampton Docks. At the very end, separated by just an iron fence, the berths can be seen. When the most famous liners and cruise ships are in port they can be seen and photographed from this wonderful vantage point. Adjoining this park is the Mayflower Monument.

On Platform Road is Queens Park. Among the greenery here is the monument to General Gordon of Khartoum.

Southampton has many other open spaces, the largest of which is the Common. This is known to so many for its lakes and children's paddling pool as well as being a popular place for dog walkers.

Peartree Green on Peartree Avenue is another well-known open space, again used by local children for playing sports and other games. There is a beautiful old church and the green overlooks the River Itchen as it makes its way down towards the Itchen Bridge.

Titanic Remembered

Wednesday 11 April 2012, the day after the opening of the SeaCity Museum, I had the enormous pleasure of attending the *Titanic* Walk. This was put on by the Sarah Siddons' fan club and members of the Point Youth Theatre, a group of very talented players of all ages who act out historical events in and around the Southampton area.

It had been 100 years since RMS *Titanic* set off on her maiden voyage to New York. She was mostly crewed by men from Southampton, many of whom lost their lives in the ensuing disaster when *Titanic* struck an iceberg. The ship was thought to be unsinkable and this tragedy savaged Southampton as so many families lost husbands, brothers and sons.

I didn't quite know what to expect as I made my way to the ruined church of Holyrood for the walk. In pouring rain we began with the dramatic reconstruction. Women were dressed in period costume, being addressed by a bishop, with girls in the pinafore dresses of the period and young boys in the clothes of their generation. Placards displayed news of the exciting, forthcoming departure of the ship from this port.

Imagine watching her sail away, from a position around the General Gordon monument in Queens Park with a view of the docks where *Titanic* was moored, to the tragedy and its aftermath, particularly the part played by the Mayor of Southampton in 1912. Alderman Henry Bowyer set up the relief fund that did so much to help bereaved families of the men lost on *Titanic*. He died, aged forty-eight in 1915 and is buried, along with many other notable men, in the Old Cemetery on Southampton Common.

The whole event was not only entertaining but also very informative. I thought I knew most of the facts about *Titanic* after being interested in her for so many years, but this was like being taken right back to the time of the ship and seeing it all from a fresh perspective.

Southampton's new SeaCity Museum was opened to the public at 12 p.m. on Tuesday 10 April, 2012. One hundred years to the day and the exact time the *Titanic* left this port to start her maiden voyage to New York. It was opened by two Southampton schoolboys William and Henry Ward who were aged 8 and 6 and whose great-grandfather George Kemish was a crew member of *Titanic* who survived the disaster. They were helped by the presence of double Olympic gold medal-winning rower James Cracknell.

Over 600 children paraded through the streets carrying placards with names and pictures of crew members from the *Titanic*. The museum is a great credit to this city. It has two floors and *Titanic*'s story unfolds on both levels. So much interest is still being shown in this story and walking around this new attraction, which also details Southampton's maritime history, made me proud once again to be a citizen of this important city.

Some people have complained that the museum spoils the look of our Civic Centre, but right from the start of building I have never agreed with this. The *Titanic* tragedy brought much sorrow and hardship to so many families here but the ship herself has never been out of people's thoughts, and not just here in Southampton. Belfast, where she was built, has its own museum and around the world the name of *Titanic* is well known.

So many visitors came to SeaCity Museum during the first few days of its opening and many more will follow as the years pass. Will *Titanic* ever be forgotten? Not by people like myself who grew up in Southampton and knew of her from a very early age. Look at the visitors; see how many children are visiting; the next generation have the interest and wonder in this ship and her fate. Lying far away on the bottom of the Atlantic Ocean, long may her memory live and Southampton will certainly never forget her.

Then & Now

The top image sums up Southampton perfectly for me. The floating bridge brings back memories of my childhood, when my firends and I crossed the River Itchen this way. It was so exciting for us all.

The bottom image shows the same spot today. It has changed a great deal, gone is the floating bridge, replaced by the new Itchen Bridge.

Shopping

The Marlands Shopping Centre

Marlands Centre was opened on 5 September 1991 by
Mrs Gail Ronson, wife of the head of Heron International,
the original developers of the centre. For me the wonder of
shopping indoors was both exciting but sad at the same time.

When I was growing up the city had the most magnificent
Rose Garden facing the front of the Civic Centre. The
fountain lit up the night skies with ever changing colours as
the water rose and fell. This has since been moved and can
now be found opposite Watts Park outside the city's main
library and art gallery. Behind Rose Garden was the Grand
Theatre, and what joy I found there in my youth. Further
in were the Hants and Dorset Bus Station and many small
shops including Plested Pies. This was all bulldozed to make
room for the Marlands Shopping Centre. So although it was
goodbye to many places and fond memories, I think the
people of this city were happy to swap it all for the comfort
of shopping in the Marlands.

I had the pleasure of meeting the present manger of the
centre, Mr Arnold Catterall his office sitting directly over
where the old bus station used to be. The main retail unit
now hosts Matalan, selling clothing and household goods on
two floor levels. There is also a Pound Shop, Disney store and
many clothes outlets. Cafés are to be found on both floors
and if jewellery is your interest this is well represented in
the centre as well.

Exiting the centre on Portland Terrace you can cross over to
Asda, the only supermarket at present in the city centre. I
use this store many times during each week, always coming
through the Marlands first, sometimes stopping to shop here
as well. As a convenient and quick route back up to the main
high street from Asda, this ensures the Marlands Centre is
usually quite busy.

West Quay Shopping Centre

Opened nine years after the Marlands, this is the largest of Southampton's shopping centres. It has around 800,000 square feet and at least 100 shopping outlets. The two anchor stores are John Lewis and Marks and Spencer. Construction began in 1997 and two of Southampton's well-known buildings had to be demolished to make way for it.

The *Echo* building was beautiful with large pillars at the front, a balcony and a large clock on the wall so shoppers in the high street could keep an eye on the time. Known and admired by many it nonetheless had to go to make way for the main entrance to the centre. The *Echo* is now printed at a new site at Redbridge. Also demolished was the factory of Pirelli General Cable Works on Portland Terrace.

Besides the anchor stores this centre provides just about everything needed from fashion, food and jewellery to mobile phones and electrical goods. Always busy, it is a wonder to me how so many shops can be contained under one roof. Waterstones have a large store here covering two floors whilst the top level is devoted to food outlets. Anything from fast food to a sit-down meal can be obtained here and the view over Southampton Docks and the surrounding area is fantastic. Many times entertainment is put on at West Quay, from bands playing to entertainments for families and children. Shopping in this centre, although sometimes hard because of the huge crowds that use it, is an enjoyable experience and many people stop here not just to shop but to meet up with friends for coffee and refreshment.

Murders Through the Ages

The Portswood Tragedy

I start with this terrible crime because it took place on the road on which I spent my childhood. Angelina Faithful was murdered by her lover Frederic Burden at No. 9 Brooklyn Road in 1896 because of her prostitution. She had left her husband and set-up home with Burden, but he was unable to reconcile himself with her professional relationships, and she made no secret of them to him. Finally losing patience with her, he took a knife and stabbed her to death in the front bedroom of the house. Her body was discovered the next day by eleven-year-old Sarah Philpot who ran errands for Angelina.

Burden had run off but was found and brought to trial at Winchester Assizes where his first trial ended without the jury reaching a verdict. At the second trial however, Burden was found guilty, sentenced to death and then hanged at Winchester gaol. The road was renamed Belgrave Road and I had many happy years growing up there until the late 1960s when the houses were all bulldozed. The area is now an industrial estate.

The Murder of Gay Gibson

The murder of Gay Gibson took place in 1947 aboard the Union Castle liner *Durban Castle*. Eileen Isabella Ronnie Gibson, known as 'Gay' Gibson, was a shorthand typist with an ambition to go on stage. Her first big break came as she played the lead role in the film *The Man with a Load of Mischief*, which was first shown in South Africa. She was returning home as a first-class passenger and had cabin B126 on B deck.

On the night of 17 October, after dancing with friends, Gay went to her cabin. Afterwards alarm bells began to ring to summon the stewards. Responding to the call, the steward on duty found another steward, James Camb, already in attendance. Camb assured him that everything was under control, but he had no right be in the cabin in the first place. The next day Gay was nowhere to be found on board, so the captain turned the ship round and made a search for her. Camb was interviewed and eventually admitted that he had been invited into Gay Gibson's cabin for sex, but he claimed that she had some kind of seizure and subsequently died. The full story was very different and showed that Camb had forced himself on Miss Gibson, as scratches on his neck and arms showed.

The real fate of this lady was that Camb panicked when he saw that she was dead and pushed her body through the porthole of the cabin into the sea below, where it was never found. He was spared the death penalty, but only because it was being considered for abolition. He did, however, spend the next twelve years in prison for the murder.

Lillian Levine – The Vital Thumbprint

The grisly murder of the lady who ran a second-hand shop at No. 51 St Mary's Road took place in 1956. The author of *Southampton Murder Victims* Jim Brown was on the murder squad that investigated this crime, and it is one I remember very well myself. I had left school at the end of 1955 and as a fifteen-year-old lad was just starting out on the great adventure of going to work and earning my own living. I was grown-up, or so I thought anyway.

I had been in the St Mary's area and passed this particular shop on many occasions, but never had any reason to go inside, until just before Christmas 1955. I wanted to buy a clock I saw in the window, to give to my mother as a present. But when I enquired about it the lady told me it didn't work. She then said she only bought clocks and watches that were broken. That ended my interest and I left the shop without delay.

So I was as shocked as the rest of this city when news broke in 1956 that the elderly lady who ran it had been found dead in the back room of the shop with shocking injuries. I can now quote from Jim Brown's book that the only real lead the police had was an unidentified thumbprint found on a cash box. Exhaustive enquiries eventually led to Gurdial Singh, a farmer from the Punjab who was living as a lodger in a bungalow in Mortimer Road, Woolston. Brought to justice despite protests at his innocence, that thumbprint matched his own and condemned him to the death penalty; he was later reprieved and his sentence was commuted to life imprisonment.

Ghostly Tales

The Campus Ghost

The Avenue Campus of Southampton University in Highfield Road was home to a former tram shed. This old building, which I believe is now demolished, was said to have been constructed on the site of an old burial ground. This may

account for the stories of unusual activity within it. It has been claimed that the old shed was haunted by the ghost of a lady, and a member of staff claimed to have seen a pair of hands protruding from underneath one of the toilet cubicles. Night staff reported hearing sounds of heavy footsteps in the shed when they knew that it was empty. Are these the restless spirits of former employees? Or the angry souls of those buried there in times gone by?

God's House Tower

There are reports of ghostly movements outside the doors of God's House Tower, situated near Southampton's Town Quay. A former prison amongst other things, this ancient building has a long history. But how can anyone explain the sounds of screams that have been heard and the clashing of swords? Could it be related to this unique story? The following is taken from a copy of the parish notes of St Julian's; it was found in the archives of the Civic Centre in Southampton.

In 1554, Prince Phillip of Spain travelled to England to marry Queen Mary. He arrived in Southampton aboard his ship as part of the Armada and was stopped, as a precaution, in Southampton Water. The sight of this fleet of Spanish ships was unsettling to the soldiers on guard at the tower. The Spanish anchored in the channel but Phillip, bored with the journey and wanting to see the sights of Southampton, was rowed ashore by the captain's son. He spent the afternoon roaming the streets and then paid a visit to the church.

Inside, he spotted a maiden and instantly fell in love with her. He followed the girl outside into the garden where he fell on her, singing her praises and asking for a dalliance.
She, however, realising who he was, pleaded with him to leave her alone. A dalliance with the future king of England could cost her life. In fear, she ran out of the gate from the garden that used to face the front door of God's House Tower. The prince was surprised however when she ran straight back in; someone else had recognised him, and there were two ruffians waiting outside to waylay him. Drawing his sword, the prince bounded through the gate and a sword fight ensued in which one of the ruffians was killed by a thrust through the heart, the other one then ran off.

Is this the sound that can now be heard outside the tower, this sword fight being re-enacted? And who was the maiden the prince fell for that day? It is believed she was the daughter of a wealthy merchant and her name was Charlotte Tyrell. I wonder if this is anything to do with the Tyrell & Green family business that was for so long situated at the town junction and has now moved into West Quay Shopping Centre as John Lewis.

SOUTHAMPTON OLD BOWLING GREEN

Established Prior 1299

"THE OLDEST BOWLING GREEN IN THE WORLD"

VISITORS WELCOME

Donated By Sir David Priestley

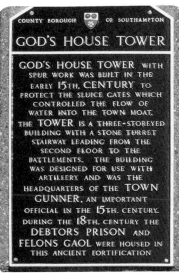

COUNTY BOROUGH OF SOUTHAMPTON

GOD'S HOUSE TOWER

GOD'S HOUSE TOWER WITH SPUR WORK WAS BUILT IN THE EARLY 15TH. CENTURY TO PROTECT THE SLUICE GATES WHICH CONTROLLED THE FLOW OF WATER INTO THE TOWN MOAT. THE TOWER IS A THREE-STOREYED BUILDING WITH A STONE TURRET STAIRWAY LEADING FROM THE SECOND FLOOR TO THE BATTLEMENTS. THE BUILDING WAS DESIGNED FOR USE WITH ARTILLERY AND WAS THE HEADQUARTERS OF THE TOWN GUNNER, AN IMPORTANT OFFICIAL IN THE 15TH. CENTURY. DURING THE 18TH. CENTURY THE DEBTORS PRISON AND FELONS GAOL WERE HOUSED IN THIS ANCIENT FORTIFICATION

A to Z of Southampton

A … Airport – Wide Lane Swaythling

B … Bargate – the former gateway to the city

C … Civic Centre

D … Dell – the former home of Southampton Football Club

E … Echo building – formerly in the High Street on the site of West Quay Shopping Centre

F … Fair on the Common three times a year

G … Graffiti – from the French troops held in the now Maritime Museum as prisoners during the Napoleonic war

H … Hoglands Park

I … Itchen Bridge

J … Jane Auten, resident from 1807–1809

K … Kingsland Market in St Mary's, replaced by Friday and Saturday markets below Bargate

L … Lordshill housing estate

M … Marlands Shopping Centre

N … Newtown – an area in the Northam and St Mary's District

O … Ordnance Survey – they moved their headquarters to Southampton in 1841

P … Panic when Southampton was sacked in 1338, it was never the same again after this

Q … Queens

R … Rose Gardens formerly facing the Civic Centre

S … Southampton Docks

T … *Titanic* memorials

U … Upper Bugle Street

V … Vosper Thornycroft, now moved to Portsmouth

W … West Quay shopping Centre

X … Xerox in London Road

Y … YMCA

Z … Zoo formerly on Southampton Common, now the Urban Wildlife Centre

QUEEN VICTORIA

QUEEN MARY 2

QUEEN ELIZABETH

Local Characters

Peddler Jack
He was the knife and scissors man who walked the streets from the Bargate to the Pier, sharpening knives and scissors for residents.

The Flower Lady Violet Smith
I never knew this lady or bought flowers from her. But saw many times, when walking down East Street or going in and out of the Debenhams department store, once known as Edwin Jones; she was always there with her flower cart. This remarkable lady, with her ever-present smile that lit up the area around her, was an inspiration in her own right as she brought joy into so many lives. She was there in all weathers and would help anyone at any time. Her blooms and her personality transformed a corner of East Street that now lies empty. Southampton lost someone who was very well loved when she sadly died in 2011.

The Guitar Man of Tyrell & Greens
There was a tunnel right through the huge department store of Tyrell & Green, now trading as John Lewis in West Quay. This pathway led from the High Street out into Palmerston Park behind. On a daily basis the Guitar Man was there, playing his guitar and collecting coins from the many passers-by. A real character, he was also very good and I, like many, stopped to listen to him more than once.

Ted Martin the Alcoholic Butcher

I knew Ted very well. My mother bought our family meat from him and I worked as his butcher's boy for three years. One of my duties was to run down to the Brook Inn on the corner of Belgrave Road several times a day for his 'medicine' or rather a double double-gin. Though well intoxicated, he never really made any mistakes as he cut up the meat and served his customers. Always outrageous with the many women who came into the shop this man taught me a great deal about life.

Rag-and-Bone Men

The call would rent the air as many rag-and-bone men plied their trade on the streets of Southampton. This was an ideal way to rid oneself of unwanted clothes and household items. Southampton had many versions of Steptoe & Son.

Spitfire Monument

The plane that did so much to save this country from German occupation, bringing eventual victory to the Allied forces, originated in Southampton. The designer was R.J. Mitchell and the Spitfire he dreamt up was built in Woolston. Because it was such a threat to Nazi Germany the Luftwaffe tried everything they could to destroy the Supermarine factory that was producing it. They failed in this endeavour, despite bombing the factory to the ground, production carried on. Parts of the plane were put together in small workshops and even garages around the city, and it continued to be flown by our brave RAF pilots.

For so long the people of Southampton have been asking for a permanent monument to be erected. A replica Spitfire can be seen at Southampton Airport, but the city needed something more imposing to remind us all of its importance. A nationwide competition was organised by the Spitfire Tribute Foundation. Invitations went out for designers to send in their plans and Nick Hancock was victorious. And no wonder, for he has designed a fitting tribute that will be placed at the site of Trafalgar Dock. Here it will be seen by the thousands of visitors as they sail into Southampton on board the cruise liners. Completion date for this wonderful monument is unknown at this time as the project is relying on private donations and will take a year to construct. I am just one of the many residents of this city who simply can't wait to see it. During the war many boys dreamt of flying one, shooting down German bombers before they could reach their intended destinations. And Nick Hancock has captured that moment just after the call of Squadron Scramble when so many Spitfires quite literally did reach for the sky.

Things I Like About Southampton

The fact I can fly from Southampton Airport or sail out of Southampton Docks or leave from Southampton Central railway station, and travel to anywhere in the world easily.

The parks and open spaces of this great city make it one of the greenest cities in the country. Southampton Common is my particular favourite. This is where I learned to swim in the children's paddling pool. The flora and fauna is wonderful and the lakes are out of this world. Add Southampton old cemetery with all its history, so well kept by the friends of the cemetery, and this large expanse of open land is a wonder enjoyed by so many of Southampton's residents.

Museums such as Tudor House and the new SeaCity Museum are both marvellous places to visit and when you walk the old walls of Southampton you take a step back into history.

The views I get from my home that looks out over Southampton Docks, with its cruise terminal and large container berths. Many times I wake up in the morning to the sight of giant cruise liners berthed seemingly just across the road. And when one or more of the three big Cunard liners are in I can see them as well. As an ex-seaman these views are priceless.

Things I Hate About Southampton

Like so many towns and cities around the country Southampton has many clubs that stay open until the early hours of the morning. This leads to large numbers of drunken people making their noisy way home. Alcohol-fuelled trouble often occurs and keeps the police busy on a nightly basis.

The closure of the city's ice rink in 1988 was disappointing. Plans are constantly being put forward for a new one to be built. These have always looked promising, but each time they have eventually been rejected.

The closure of essential services in the city, such as police stations and post offices, as well as many services for vulnerable people of all ages. This is causing concern and anxiety.

People who illegally ride bicycles through the precinct on Above Bar, resulting in pedestrians having to jump out of their way.

Local Dialect

Mush … The name used by people of other counties for Southampton residents born in the city

Sherricking … Being well and truly told off

Shrammed … Feeling extremely cold

Winty … Weather that is cold, wet or windy

Safty … This afternoon

Fiosty … Anything that is damp and musty

Southampton dialect tends to leave off aitches and the word 'my' is pronounced as 'me'. A good description of this was when a colleague of mine told me about a function he attended where there were hooks in the hall for hats and coats. He apparently, hung his hat on the hook in the hall, but what he actually said was: I 'ung me 'at on the 'ook in the 'all.

The Diamond Jubilee of Queen Elizabeth II

Just before 5 a.m. on the morning of Tuesday, 5 May 2012, Southampton resounded to the sound of ships' whistles announcing the arrival in port of three of Cunard's liners, all bearing royal names. To celebrate our sovereign Queen's Diamond Jubilee, *Queen Mary 2*, *Queen Elizabeth* and *Queen Victoria* sailed majestically up Southampton Water to spend a day in their home port. This was the first time that all three of these magnificent ships were here together and it crowned a day of celebration. Despite appalling weather, many turned out to enjoy a party atmosphere in Mayflower Park. The fun went on all day and was topped by the most magnificent fireworks display as all three prepared to depart later in the evening.

This is the sort of event that makes being born and raised in Southampton so rewarding.

Howards' Way

The very popular programme *Howards' Way*, which ran from 1985 to 1990 was filmed in Burseldon and Hamble as well as scenes in Fareham, Lee-on-the Solent and Southampton. A hugely popular programme about a boatbuilding yard and the conflicts of its owners, it starred, amongst others: Maurice Colbourne, Jan Harvey, Stephen Yardley, Glyn Owen, and Tony Anholt as well as an impressive list of more big-name stars. During its run, *Howards' Way* brought so much pleasure to so many viewers and also put Burseldon and Hamble in the forefront of so many people's minds.

Youngstar TV and Film School

The Youngstar TV and Film School is a school that makes films with children from the ages of five to eighteen, from all over the City of Southampton. Local writer Sandra Philip writes scripts from the students' own ideas and films are shot from locations all over Southampton.

There is a premiere once a year that is held at the Harbour Lights Cinema at Ocean Village. Here the students, with their friends and families, attend a magnificent Hollywood-style screening of all the films they have made over the year. In 2012 these include: *Children of the Wood*, a horror that was filmed in Telegraph Wood in West End Southampton and *Darton High*, a fictional soap filmed on location at Redbridge Community School.

Established in 2002, Youngstar has produced thirty short films in the ten years since opening and all have featured local children. Southampton can be proud of this company that gives children the chance to live their dreams and star in films and soaps. Some may go on and make acting their career and in this way make the City of Southampton proud that more of its young people are making their mark in the world of entertainment.

Politics

Southampton is currently divided into two Parliamentary constituencies solely covering the City: the Itchen on one side and the Test on the other. However, two of the City's electoral wards – Bassett and Swaythling – lie within the Romsey and Southampton North constituency, previously represented by the Liberal Democrats' Sandra Gidley until the 2010 general election where it was won by the Conservative candidate Caroline Nokes.

The current parliamentary boundary review recommendations suggest that the present boundaries will remain except in the case of the Swaythling ward, where it is proposed that it should transfer to the Southampton Test constituency.

Southampton Itchen

The Southampton Itchen Parliamentary constituency covers the eastern part of the city including areas like Bitterne, Harefield, Sholing and Woolston amongst others. It also encompasses the Bargate ward on the western side of the River Itchen (which includes neighbourhoods in the St Mary's, Ocean Village, Holyrood, Old Town and Polygon areas).

This was always considered a safe Labour seat until 1983 when the Conservative MP Christopher Chope won it and held until 1992. The only other time since the 1950s when this seat was not in Labour's hands was when Bob Mitchell won it after a by-election in 1971. However, he went over to the SDP in 1981. Labour regained it in 1992 when the now-former cabinet minister John Denham narrowly defeated Christopher Chope. John Denham has held the seat ever since; albeit he only secured it by the narrowest of margins in 2010, a mere 192 votes.

Since 1950 this seat has been held by:

1950: Ralph Mooney – Labour

1955: Dr Horace King – Labour

1965: Dr Horace King – Speaker

1971: Bob Mitchell – Labour

1981: Bob Mitchell – SDP

1983: Christopher Chope – Conservative

1992, 1997, 2001, 2005, 2010: John Denham – Labour

John Denham currently represents this constituency.

Southampton Test

The Southampton Test Parliamentary constituency seat covers the western part of the city and was created in 1950 when the former two-member Southampton Constituency was abolished.

It covers the electoral wards of: Bevois (comprising the Bevois Town, Nicholstown and Northam neighbourhoods); Coxford (comprising the Lordshill, Lordswood and Aldermoor neighbourhoods); Freemantle (also including the Banister Park neighbourhood and a small part of Shirley); Millbrook (also including the Maybush and Regents Park neighbourhoods); Portswood (also including the St Denys and Highfield neighbourhoods); Redbridge and Shirley (comprising the Old Shirley, Shirley Warren, and Upper Shirley neighbourhoods).

MPs for this seat have been:

1950: Horace King – Labour

1955: John Howard – Conservative

1964: John Fletcher-Cooke – Conservative

1966: Bob Mitchell – Labour

1970: James Hill – Conservative

Oct 1974: Bryan Gould – Labour

1979: James Hill – Conservative

1997, 2001, 2005, 2010: Dr Alan Whitehead – Labour.

This shows a mix of MPs from both Labour and Conservative parties having held this seat, but the present incumbent, Dr Alan Whitehead, has successfully retained it since his first victory in 1997. At the 2010 General Election he held it with a majority of 2,413 votes.

The Saints

Founded in 1885, Southampton Football Club has ecclesiastical origins, being originally called St Mary's Church of England Young Men's Association (or St Mary's YMA). The Saints, as they are nicknamed, were one of the founding clubs of the Premier League, but suffered relegation in 2005 after twenty-seven years in top-flight football. Following their drop, the club saw many years of fractious boardroom mismanagement and suffered a slide down to League 1. During this time, the discontent over the chairmanship of the club raged on with the fans wanting to rid the club of its then chairman, who they had no faith in whatsoever. Despite several potential bids and various companies showing interest in taking over at St Mary's, the club almost went out of business. Thankfully Swiss multimillionaire Markus Leibherr saved the day in the summer of 2009. Now the club flourishes again in the Premier League and has manager Nigel Atkins at the helm. Sadly Mr Leibherr died in August 2010, before he could see his dream of getting the Saints back to the Premiership realised. But now that they are, the St Mary's Stadium erupts once more to the joyful tones of 'When the Saints go Marching In'.

Hampshire Cricket Club

Among the famous and wonderfully gifted cricketers who played for Hampshire County Cricket Club were men such as Gorden Greenidge, a great opening batsman who played in a successful West Indies Test team. He played for Hampshire from 1970 to 1987. Another great was a second West Indies player, the exciting bowler Roy Marshall. He played for the club and wowed many supporters from 1953 to 1972. Sadly he passed away in the early 1990s. The South African batsman Barry Richards graced the playing surfaces of the old County Ground in 1968. And of course every Hampshire fan will remember with such fondness the days when the club was under the captaincy of the world's greatest spin bowler, the unbelievable Shane Warne.

The County Ground, not far from the Dell, on Northlands Road, was small and was home to Hampshire County Cricket Club. They have also moved, and now reside at the large and magnificent Rose Bowl in West End. This ground is being talked of as one of the most superb in the country. England played One Day Internationals here; against Australia in 2009 and both Australia and West Indies in 2010. On 16 June 2011 the ground hosted its first Test match. England took on Sri Lanka and the match was drawn. The Rose Bowl has recently been renamed and is now known as the Ageas Bowl.

Infamous for ...

Southampton was featured in a sad case of murder on the high seas in 1884. The small yacht *Mignonette* foundered while on its way to Australia, and the captain, with two seamen and a seventeen-year-old cabin boy took to the lifeboat. The boy, who came from Itchen Ferry Village Southampton, was Richard Parker. With no food or water in the boat the three men, Captain Tom Dudley, Edwin Stephens and Edmond Brooks, killed the young boy in order to eat his flesh and drink his blood. They did this for their own survival. After the killing all three of these men were picked up and it was obvious to the rescuers, on seeing the human remains in the boat, what had occurred. This was when British law changed. Unfortunate incidents like this had taken place before, but it was never looked on as murder, rather as the sacrifice of one life in order to save many more. The three men in this case though did go to court to face a charge of murder and were convicted of the crime. Queen Victoria eventually granted them a pardon after they each spent six months in prison.

Richard Parker is remembered in the part of Southampton that was once known as Itchen Ferry Village. It is now Peartree Avenue and in the beautiful church that overlooks Peartree Green is a tombstone with the name of Richard Parker and the reference to his fate all those years ago.

Richard Parker was killed and eaten by Tom Dudley and Edwin Stephens to prevent starvation.

Regina versus Dudley and Stephens (1884) established the precedent that necessity is no defence against a charge of murder.

Seasons

Spring is eagerly anticipated in Southampton every year as the parks that are so superbly tended break into a wonderful sight. The flower beds burst with colour as the different varieties reach their peak. The gardeners show such skill, co-ordinating the different colours so they complement each other perfectly. The parks and green spaces are truly a joy to see.

 But on the night of 15 October 1987, during the Great Storm that ripped through the south of England some of these beds were damaged. Many of the trees lining the avenues around the city were also brought crashing to the ground. This was the most devastating storm in my experience and in many of my fellow Sotonians as well.

Piracy on the High Seas

The beautiful village of Hamble, which lies on the River Hamble, is best known today because of the Motor Museum and Palace House, the home of Lord Montague. But centuries ago this was a thriving shipbuilding area. Tales abound of pirates who raided here and at other places in and around Southampton.

The year 1338 was a devastating time for Southampton. The town was attacked by the French Navy as well as pirates; silver, wine and other items were plundered and Southampton lost many of its citizens too. But this sacking of the town did not go unpunished and the British rallied and set sail for France. Revenge was swift and many French towns and villages were attacked and burned.

The raid on Southampton was successful because the walls of the town were in a state of disrepair. After the French and pirate raids, the walls were repaired and fortified so that nothing like this could ever happen again.

Sir Walter Raleigh and Sir Francis Drake are not names that roll off the tongue when talking about Southampton, yet history tells us that both these men were here and that goods from their ships along with money from privateers helped save the town.

Websites

www.southampton.gov.uk

www.visit-southampton.co.uk

www.southampton.ac.uk

www.thearthousesouthampton.co.uk

www.saintsfc.co.uk

www.southamptoncitycentre.co.uk

www.southamptoncitymission.co.uk

http://southamptoncityscouts.co.uk

www.seacitymuseum.co.uk

https://southampton.bravosolution.co.uk

The Future

The future plans for Southampton's development are interesting, if not to say exciting. But they are simply plans at the moment. Most of the city's residents are waiting for news of the development of the old Royal Pier. This has crumbled into complete ruin and parts of it have collapsed altogether. It is now seen as an eyesore by Sotonians, who worry that so many people from all parts of the UK and other visitors who arrive aboard the many huge cruise and passenger liners get this as their first look at the city of Southampton. The opposite images, though over two years old now, show what this part of the city could be developed into. Although it has to be stressed that nothing at this time has been decided and this is just a pointer towards what could take shape.

There are many new buildings already in place and the future of the city does indeed look to be bright. From a boy who grew up among the ruins of the city after the Second World War and who played in the many bombsites around Southampton, I have to say the city is now a place to be proud of.

What Southampton means to me

I can sum this up in just one word: Everything. It has been my home since I was born in late December 1940, right up until today. I have, of course, been away a few times, but wherever that has been Southampton has always been with me. It beats through my veins and a picture of it stays in my brain wherever I am in the world. The Second World War was raging as I made my entrance into the world and my hometown was a target for our foes. But once peace was gained once more I, like the rest of my siblings, came out from behind the protection of my mother and the air-raid shelter and started out on a journey of discovery in and around what was then the town of Southampton. There were bombed-out buildings everywhere and so many of these became a playground for eager boys. But the sheer beauty of this wonderful town was not lost on any of us. The town itself prospered as it started to recover from the war damage and took on its look as an important maritime town. The two most beautiful ships in the world then came and went from the docks, so we saw the elegance and wonder of the *Queen Mary* and her sister *Queen Elizabeth* so many times.

During my teenage years Southampton became a city (1964) and grew into the place it is today.

The first time I left my home town behind and slept in a different county was in 1957, when I went to the National Sea Training School, *Vindicatrix*, in Sharpness, Gloucestershire. Here I came into contact with boys my own age, but from many parts of the British Isles. They asked me where I was from and I proudly said Southampton. 'Oh, you're a mush are you?' was the disdainful reply. It hurt me because of the contempt I heard in their voices for a city none of them had even visited before. But following the course, many of them came here in order to ship-out for the Merchant Navy, and more than one of them stayed and made their home here.

I can sum this up with the simple words that I am a Sotonian through and through and will always be. I was born here and I will die here, and when that happens part of this city will still be embedded in my soul.

Things to do in Southampton – Checklist

Walk the city walls. ☐

Take in a game at St Mary's Stadium. ☐

Have a picnic on the Common. ☐

See the Spitfire memorial. ☐

Visit the SeaCity Museum. ☐

Take in a play at the Nuffield Theatre. ☐

Visit the medieval Red Lion pub in High Street. ☐

Visit the historic docks. ☐

Take a trip down Southampton Water to the Isle of Wight on a ferry. ☐

See the *Titanic* memorial. ☐

See the residents of the Urban Wildlife Centre. ☐

Take a moment of reflection in the ancient Church of St Michael. ☐

Picture Credits

Unless otherwise stated, all images are copyright of the author, or copyright free.

Page:

7. Royston Smith (Courtesy of Royston Smith)

9. Itchen Bridge (Courtesy of the Julie Green collection)

19. Le Havre port. (Courtesy of Urban)

Qingdao Bay, China. (Courtesy of Allen Wang)

21. Southampton Port. (Courtesy of JCB photography) Fawley Oil Refinery. (Courtesy of Exxon Mobile)

23. The Oxford Arms. (Courtesy of Penny Legg)

The Grapes. (Courtesy of the Julie Green collection)

27. Polygon Hotel; Grand Theatre; Last Tram through the Bargate. (Courtesy of the Julie Green collection)

31. SeaCity Museum. (Courtesy of the SeaCity Museum)

33. Wool House, former site of the maritme museum. (Courtesy of the Julie Green collection)

39. Brian Hooper and Jeff Henry. (Courtesy of Brian Hooper)

43. Balloon Festival; Boat show. (Courtesy of the Julie Green collection)

47. Spitfire plaque; Queen Victoria. (Courtesy of the Julie Green collection)

49. Provident Building. (Courtesy of the Julie Green collection)

53. The Bosuns Locker Pub; Jane Austen plaque. (Courtesy of the Julie Green collection)

55. Craig David. (Courtesy of Jonathan Andel)

57. Chris Packham. (Courtesy of McGeddon)

59. Isaac Watts statue; Tower Monument. (Courtesy of the Julie Green collection)

If you enjoyed this book, you may also be interested in …

Growing up in Wartime Southampton

JAMES MARSH

Born in the first year of the Second World War, James Marsh had a turbulent infancy. Here you will read his story as he grew up in the most unsettled decades of the twentieth century.

978 0 7524 5840 3

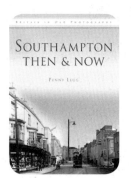

Southampton Then & Now

PENNY LEGG

A stunning pictorial history of Southampton contrasting a rare selection of archive images with full-colour modern photographs, this book reveals the ever-changing faces and buildings of the city.

978 0 7524 5693 5

Visit our website and discover thousands of other History Press books.

www.thehistorypress.co.uk

The History Press